5th Grade

Algebra

Workbook

Belongs to:

....

....

....

Grade 5 Math Workbook
With Answers

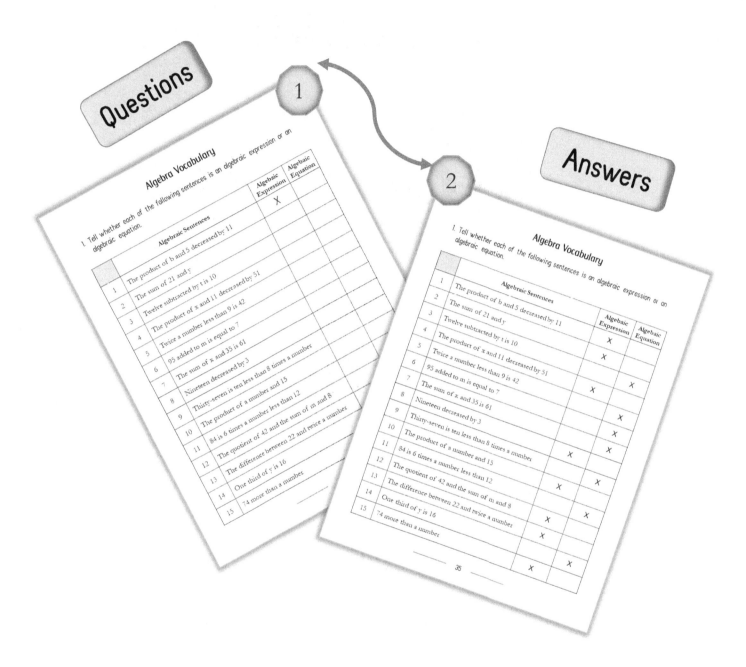

Questions

1

Answers

2

Please share your appreciated comments
with us via our Amazon page:
Wisconsin Oliver Madi

Content

Algebra Vocabulary

1. Determine the constant(s) and the variable(s) in each algebraic expression.

	Algebraic Expressions	Constant(s)	Variable(s)
1	c + 13	13	c
2	10 - b		
3	7 + m		
4	3q + 1		
5	18p		
6	5 + d + a		
7	51		
8	$\dfrac{m}{5}$		
9	$\dfrac{11}{t} - b$		
10	$\dfrac{6}{a}$		
11	8xy + 31		
12	47 + m + 9		
13	x + 3		
14	63 + x − 11b		
15	$\dfrac{5}{4}(m + p)$		

Algebra Vocabulary

1. Tell whether the following is an algebraic expression or an algebaic equation.

	Algebraic (Expressions and Equations)	Algebaic Expression	Algebaic Equation
1	$3 + 2x$	X	
2	$6b = 2$		
3	$25 - 9c$		
4	$7a - 22 = 11$		
5	$102 = 4y - 3$		
6	$5x - 17 = 18 + 54x$		
7	$8a - 5$		
8	$\dfrac{t}{13} = 77$		
9	$\dfrac{x + 1}{2} - 35$		
10	$\dfrac{6a}{5} + 9 = 3a$		
11	$5p = 2p - 1$		
12	$x^2 - 3$		
13	$1 = 2 - y^2$		
14	$\dfrac{x + 1}{2}$		
15	$\dfrac{5x}{4} + 3 = 0$		

Algebra Vocabulary

1. Tell whether each of the following sentences is an algebraic expression or an algebraic equation.

	Algebraic Sentences	Algebaic Expression	Algebraic Equation
1	The product of b and 5 decreased by 11	X	
2	The sum of 21 and y		
3	Twelve subtracted by t is 10		
4	The product of x and 11 decreased by 51		
5	Twice a number less than 9 is 42		
6	95 added to m is equal to 7		
7	The sum of x and 35 is 61		
8	Nineteen decreased by 3		
9	Thirty-seven is ten less than 8 times a number		
10	The product of a number and 15		
11	84 is 6 times a number less than 12		
12	The quotient of 42 and the sum of m and 8		
13	The difference between 22 and twice a number		
14	One third of y is 16		
15	74 more than a number		

Evaluating Expressions with 1 Variable

1. Evaluate each of the following expressions for x = 7.

1. $x + 10 =$ __17__

2. $x + 23 =$ _____

3. $x + 11 - 5 =$ _____

4. $x - 7 =$ _____

5. $15 - x + 8 =$ _____

6. $9 + x =$ _____

7. $31 + x =$ _____

8. $x - 4 =$ _____

9. $3 + x - 2 =$ _____

10. $x + 59 =$ _____

2. Evaluate each of the following expressions for y = 12.

1. $y + 13 =$ _____

2. $y - 5 =$ _____

3. $y + 9 - 2 =$ _____

4. $y - 9 =$ _____

5. $6 + y - 8 =$ _____

6. $9 + y =$ _____

7. $25 + y =$ _____

8. $y + 33 =$ _____

9. $27 - y + 3 =$ _____

10. $67 - y =$ _____

Evaluating Expressions with 1 Variable

1. Evaluate each of the following expressions for x = 15.

1. $x - 5 =$ _____

2. $x + 10 =$ _____

3. $x - 14 - 1 =$ _____

4. $27 - x =$ _____

5. $42 - x + 20 =$ _____

6. $3 + x =$ _____

7. $73 - x =$ _____

8. $x + 2 =$ _____

9. $1 + x - 5 =$ _____

10. $x - 0 =$ _____

2. Evaluate each of the following expressions for y = 21.

1. $5 + y =$ _____

2. $96 - y - 10 =$ _____

3. $y + 11 =$ _____

4. $y + 61 - 19 =$ _____

5. $42 - y =$ _____

6. $y - 4 =$ _____

7. $39 + y + 9 =$ _____

8. $21 - y =$ _____

9. $73 - y + 15 =$ _____

10. $89 - y + 16 =$ _____

Evaluating Expressions with 1 Variable

1. Evaluate each of the following expressions for x = 3.

1. $5x =$ _____

2. $6x + 9 =$ _____

3. $2(7x) =$ _____

4. $4 + 8x =$ _____

5. $\dfrac{x}{3} =$ _____

6. $3x =$ _____

7. $7x - 4 =$ _____

8. $7(4x) =$ _____

9. $34 - 9x =$ _____

10. $\dfrac{12x}{3} + 13 =$ _____

2. Evaluate each of the following expressions for y = 4.

1. $\dfrac{8y}{2} =$ _____

2. $\dfrac{36}{y} =$ _____

3. $5 - \dfrac{y}{4} =$ _____

4. $9y + 17 =$ _____

5. $35 - \dfrac{4y}{8} =$ _____

6. $\dfrac{8}{y} =$ _____

7. $\dfrac{24}{y} =$ _____

8. $\dfrac{y}{1} + 10 =$ _____

9. $13 - 3y =$ _____

10. $10 - \dfrac{3y}{2} - 4 =$ _____

Evaluating Expressions with 1 Variable

1. Evaluate each of the following expressions for x = 2.

1. $x^2 + 1 = $ _____

2. $(3x)^2 = $ _____

3. $x^2 - 1 = $ _____

4. $46 - (3x)^2 = $ _____

5. $4x^2 + 9 = $ _____

6. $3 + x^2 = $ _____

7. $(2x)^2 + 5 = $ _____

8. $6 - x^2 = $ _____

9. $16 - (2x)^2 = $ _____

10. $3x^2 - 7 = $ _____

2. Evaluate each of the following expressions for y = 2.

1. $\dfrac{y^2}{1} = $ _____

2. $4 + 5y^2 = $ _____

3. $5y^2 - 10 = $ _____

4. $y^3 = $ _____

5. $y^3 + 4 = $ _____

6. $\dfrac{2y^2}{6} = $ _____

7. $2y^2 + 11 = $ _____

8. $\dfrac{6y^2}{3} - 5 = $ _____

9. $2y^3 = $ _____

10. $y^3 - 8 = $ _____

Evaluating Expressions with 2 Variables

1. Evaluate each of the following expressions for $x = 2$ and $y = 3$.

1. $x + y = $ _____

2. $y - x = $ _____

3. $x + y + 2 = $ _____

4. $15 + y - x = $ _____

5. $y - 3 - x = $ _____

6. $y + x = $ _____

7. $x - y = $ _____

8. $x - 2 + y = $ _____

9. $16 + x + y = $ _____

10. $y - x - 1 = $ _____

2. Evaluate each of the following expressions for $x = 4$, $y = 6$ and $z = 9$.

1. $x + z = $ _____

2. $6 + z - x = $ _____

3. $x + 51 - z = $ _____

4. $5 + (y + z) = $ _____

5. $y + x - z = $ _____

6. $z - y = $ _____

7. $23 - y = $ _____

8. $x + y + z = $ _____

9. $12 - (z - y) = $ _____

10. $x + z - y = $ _____

Evaluating Expressions with 2 Variables

1. Evaluate each of the following expressions for x = 8 and y = 2.

1. $3x + y =$ _____

2. $10y - x =$ _____

3. $4x + 3y - 20 =$ _____

4. $21 - y - 2x =$ _____

5. $\dfrac{y}{2} - 1 + x =$ _____

6. $5y + x =$ _____

7. $2x - 8y =$ _____

8. $6x - 15 + 2y =$ _____

9. $16 + \dfrac{x}{2} + 5y =$ _____

10. $\dfrac{x + y}{2} - 6 =$ _____

2. Evaluate each of the following expressions for x = 10, y = 5 and z = 7.

1. $xy =$ _____

2. $\dfrac{x}{y} =$ _____

3. $\dfrac{4y}{z - 5} =$ _____

4. $\dfrac{7x}{z} + 5 =$ _____

5. $100xz + 5 =$ _____

6. $2yz - 1 =$ _____

7. $2xy + 3 =$ _____

8. $x - 2y - 4 =$ _____

9. $\dfrac{x}{z - y} - 5 =$ _____

10. $\dfrac{xz}{y} + \dfrac{2yz}{x} =$ _____

Evaluating Expressions with 2 Variables

1. Evaluate each of the following expressions for x = 3 and y = 5.

1. $x^2 + y =$ _____

2. $5xy - 1 =$ _____

3. $2x^2 + 3y^2 =$ _____

4. $(x - y)^2 =$ _____

5. $\dfrac{x^2}{3} - 1 =$ _____

6. $5y^2 - 2x =$ _____

7. $7(2x - y) =$ _____

8. $x^2 - 1 - y^2 =$ _____

9. $100xy - 500 =$ _____

10. $\dfrac{x + y^2}{4} - 7 =$ _____

2. Evaluate each of the following expressions for x = 3, y = 12 and z = 8.

1. $2x^2y =$ _____

2. $x^3 - 40 =$ _____

3. $\dfrac{yz}{x + 1} =$ _____

4. $3x^2 + 2y - z =$ _____

5. $xyz =$ _____

6. $200xz =$ _____

7. $(2x + 3y)^2 =$ _____

8. $\dfrac{xz}{y} + \dfrac{yz}{x} =$ _____

9. $\dfrac{z^2}{x^2 - 1} - 10 =$ _____

10. $(x - y)^2 - z^2 =$ _____

Writing Algebraic Expressions

1. Determine what operation is indicated by each of the following words.

	Words	Add (+)	Subtract (−)	Multiply (X)	Divide (÷)
1)	Difference		X		
2)	Quotient				
3)	Increased by				
4)	Decreased by				
5)	Of				
6)	Sum				
7)	Subtracted from				
8)	Distributed among				
9)	Product				
10)	In addition to				
11)	Double				
12)	Less				
13)	More than				

Writing Algebraic Expressions

1. Determine what operation is indicated by each of the following words.

	Words	Add (+)	Subtract (−)	Multiply (X)	Divide (÷)
14)	Divided by				
15)	Fewer than				
16)	Total				
17)	Per				
18)	Minus				
19)	Multiplied by				
20)	Plus				
21)	Twice				
22)	Less than				
23)	Times				
24)	Take away				
25)	Into				

Writing Algebraic Expressions

1. Rewrite each of the following phrases as an algebraic expression.

	Phrase	Algebraic Expression
1.	Nine decreased by b	9 − b
2.	Eleven less than x	
3.	y increased by 5	
4.	a less than 21	
5.	x divided by 2	
6.	Ninteen multiplied by a number y	
7.	The product of 13 and f	
8.	Thirty-one less than t	

2. Rewrite each of the following phrases as an algebraic expression.

	Phrase	Algebraic Expression
1.	Five more than m	m + 5
2.	x diminished by 42	
3.	Three-fourths of y	
4.	Thrice a number x	
5.	The quotient of m and 11	
6.	The sum of 81 and d	
7.	Seventy-nine less than x	
8.	Ninety-eight more than f	

Writing Algebraic Expressions

1. Rewrite each of the following phrases as an algebraic expression.

	Phrase	Algebraic Expression
1.	The difference between m and 17	m – 17
2.	The product of 35 and x	
3.	t less than 52	
4.	x increased by y	
5.	8 times p	
6.	11 more than b	
7.	The sum of x and 63	
8.	The ratio of 22 and y	

2. Rewrite each of the following phrases as an algebraic expression.

	Phrase	Algebraic Expression
1.	Twice a number d	2d
2.	The sum of b and 46	
3.	Exceeds x by 71	
4.	The quotient of t and 92	
5.	y reduced by 21	
6.	The ratio of 18 and b	
7.	The difference between 102 and m	
8.	x less than y	

Writing Algebraic Expressions

1. Rewrite each of the following phrases as an algebraic expression.

	Phrase	Algebraic Expression
1.	The product of x and 7 increased by 12	7x + 12
2.	The quotient of y and sum of t and 4	
3.	21 greater than x	
4.	a subtracted by 10	
5.	Seventy-four increased by nine times x	
6.	Twenty-six less than three times m	
7.	Forty-seven more than Six times q	
8.	Two-thirds of p	

2. Rewrite each of the following phrases as an algebraic expression.

	Phrase	Algebraic Expression
1.	Two times y, decreased by 54	2y − 54
2.	Square of m	
3.	Nineteen decreased by the product of 4 and t	
4.	Eighty-five less than the square of x	
5.	The quotient of 22 and the sum of 15 and b	
6.	Three times the product of x and y	
7.	The sum of 21 and the quotient of t and 8	
8.	The product of 16 and square of x	

Simplifying Expressions

1. Simplify each of the following expressions.

1. $3x + x =$ ___**4x**___

2. $5x - x =$ _____

3. $4y + 7y =$ _____

4. $13x - 8x - 3x + 13 - 11 =$ _____

5. $6y - 2 + 10y + 7 - 20y - 1 =$ _____

6. $2x + 5 + x =$ _____

7. $7x + 10 - x =$ _____

8. $9x - 5x =$ _____

9. $25 - 2x + 3x =$ _____

10. $12x - 5 + 5x =$ _____

2. Simplify each of the following expressions.

1. $9 + 3y + 8 + 5y - 2 + 4y =$ _____

2. $5x + 1 + 2x + 7 - 7x - 8 =$ _____

3. $10x + 8 - 6x + 5 + 2x + 1 =$ _____

4. $4 - 5 + 2x - 4x - 6 - 9x =$ _____

5. $5x + 8x - 3x + 9 - 17 =$ _____

6. $9y + 5 - 9y =$ _____

7. $4 + 5x - 4 =$ _____

8. $19x - 21x =$ _____

9. $31x + x =$ _____

10. $-x + 22x =$ _____

Simplifying Expressions

1. Simplify each of the following expressions then evaluate it for x = 4.

1. $6x + 5x = $ ___11x___ $= $ __44__

2. $12x - 8x = $ _____ $= $ ___

3. $9x - 10x + 1 = $ _____ $= $ ___

4. $15x - 10x - 20 = $ _____ $= $ ___

5. $7x - 2 + x = $ _____ $= $ ___

6. $8 + 20x - 17x = $ _____ $= $ ___

7. $-x - 6 + 3x = $ _____ $= $ ___

8. $32x - 21x = $ _____ $= $ ___

9. $100 - 20x + 4 + = $ _____ $= $ ___

10. $18x - 12 + 2x = $ _____ $= $ ___

2. Simplify each of the following expressions then evaluate it for y = 3.

1. $21y - 7y + 15 - 3y - 7 + 12 = $ ___11y + 20___ $= $ __53__

2. $4y + 20 + 10y - 6 - 5y - 11 = $ _____ $= $ _____

3. $32y - 15 + 5y + 12 - 30y + 3 - y = $ _____ $= $ _____

4. $30 - 8y - 20 + 2y - 4y + 13 - 3 + y = $ _____ $= $ _____

5. $54y + 21 - 4y - 40 - 30y - 41 = $ _____ $= $ _____

6. $2y - 10 + 40y - 2y + 100 - 1 = $ _____ $= $ _____

7. $100y - 20 - 40 - 40y - 30y + 45 = $ _____ $= $ _____

Solving One-Step Equations

1. Solve each of the following equations. Answers should be expressed as: x = ____

1. $x + 1 = 2$; $x =$ __1__

2. $x + 5 = 10$; $x =$ ___

3. $2 + x = 16$; $x =$ ___

4. $x + 1000 = 1251$; $x =$ ___

5. $325 + x = 402$; $x =$ ___

6. $x + 100 = 250$; $x =$ ___

7. $x + 12 = 25$; $x =$ ___

8. $25 + x = 63$; $x =$ ___

9. $x + 14 = 14$; $x =$ ___

10. $47 + x = 50$; $x =$ ___

2. Solve each of the following equations. Answers should be expressed as: x = ____

1. $x - 1 = 3$; $x =$ __4__

2. $x - 9 = 1$; $x =$ ___

3. $x - 7 = 14$; $x =$ ___

4. $x - 105 = 125$; $x =$ ___

5. $x - 2500 = 55$; $x =$ ___

6. $x - 30 = 45$; $x =$ ___

7. $x - 2 = 45$; $x =$ ___

8. $x - 11 = 5$; $x =$ ___

9. $x - 1004 = 16$; $x =$ ___

10. $x - 3 = 1007$; $x =$ ___

Solving One-Step Equations

1. Solve each of the following equations. Answers should be expressed as: x = ____

1. $2x = 4$; x = __2__

2. $4x = 12$; x = ___

3. $5x = 30$; x = ___

4. $7x = 7$; x = ___

5. $10x = 400$; x = ___

6. $9x = 81$; x = ___

7. $11x = 55$; x = ___

8. $6x = 24$; x = ___

9. $3x = 90$; x = ___

10. $15x = 150$; x = ___

2. Solve each of the following equations. Answers should be expressed as: x = ___

1. $\dfrac{x}{2} = 1$; x = __2__

2. $\dfrac{x}{3} = 4$; x = ___

3. $12x = 48$; x = ___

4. $\dfrac{2x}{3} = 4$; x = ___

5. $50x = 1000$; x = ___

6. $\dfrac{x}{5} = 10$; x = ___

7. $\dfrac{3x}{7} = 6$; x = ___

8. $22x = 110$; x = ___

9. $\dfrac{14x}{3} = 28$; x = ___

10. $\dfrac{8x}{11} = 32$; x = ___

Solving 2 Step Equations

1. Solve each of the following equations and show your work.

1) $2x + 4 = 12$

2) $1 + 3x = 22$

3) $5x - 3 = 42$

4) $42 - 4x = 2$

5) $12x + 62 = 86$

6) $31 + 18x = 121$

7) $22x - 7 = 15$

8) $13x - 11 = 28$

9) $19 + 8x = 99$

10) $15x + 63 = 153$

Solving 2 Sided Equations

1. Solve each of the following equations and show your work.

1) $2x + 1 = x + 3$

2) $3x + 20 = 45 + 2x$

3) $4x - 3 = 2x + 7$

4) $x + 1 = 3 - x$

5) $10 - x = 17 - 2x$

6) $63 - 5x = 90 - 8x$

7) $2x + 21 = 29 - 2x$

8) $3 - x = 20 - 2x$

9) $92 + 6x = 112 + 4x$

10) $6 + 8x - 32 = 5x + 19$

Solving 2 Sided Equations

1. Solve each of the following equations and show your work.

1) $5 + 4x - 1 = 2x + 34$

2) $11 - 7x - 10 = 152 - 8x - 51$

3) $7 + 21x - 101 = 16x - 84$

4) $9x - 33 = 69 + 4x - 47$

5) $7x - 10 = 30 - 3x$

6) $2x - 49 + 25 = 112 + x - 87$

7) $91 + 13x - 10 = 30 - 7x + 409$

8) $100 + 125x = 3,600 + 25x$

9) $1 - x = 95 - 2x$

10) $10 + x = 2,420 - x$

Equations with 2 Variables

1. Complete each of the following tables.

1) y = x

x	y
1	1
2	
3	
4	
5	
6	
7	

2) y = x + 1

x	y
5	6
1	
7	
9	
4	
2	
8	

3) y = x + 10

x	y
5	15
1	
7	
9	
4	
2	
8	

2. Complete each of the following tables.

1) y = x − 1

x	y
2	1
11	
8	
13	
1	
5	
19	

2) y = x − 4

x	y
8	4
9	
5	
4	
12	
10	
20	

3) y = x − 12

x	y
25	13
12	
32	
17	
13	
42	
102	

Equations with 2 Variables

1. Complete each of the following tables.

1) $y = 2x$

x	y
15	30
8	
21	
35	
4	
18	
50	

2) $y = 3x + 2$

x	y
4	14
15	
42	
9	
1	
0	
16	

3) $y = 2x + 15$

x	y
31	77
10	
25	
19	
52	
8	
12	

2. Complete each of the following tables.

1) $y = 4x - 2$

x	y
2	6
9	
1	
10	
62	
85	
5	

2) $y = 5x - 20$

x	y
16	60
4	
30	
6	
44	
14	
5	

3) $y = 100x - 20$

x	y
2	180
5	
6	
1	
3	
12	
8	

Equations with 2 Variables

1. Complete each of the following tables.

1) $x + y = 16$

x	y
12	4
4	
1	
10	
6	
14	
2	

2) $y + x = 25$

x	y
20	14
12	
25	
9	
18	
5	
24	

3) $y - x = 7$

x	y
72	79
18	
4	
57	
19	
1	
95	

2. Complete each of the following tables.

1) $y - 9 = x$

x	y
29	38
10	
38	
7	
1	
13	
55	

2) $y + 6 = 2x$

x	y
4	2
63	
19	
10	
50	
8	
3	

3) $y - 2 = x + 1$

x	y
3	6
11	
50	
125	
2	
73	
83	

Equations with 2 Variables

1. Complete and determine the equation that describes each of the following tables.

1)

x	y
3	5
10	**12**
5	7
1	3
25	**27**

Equation:

$y =$ __x + 2__

2)

x	y
11	15
7	
21	25
4	8
2	

Equation:

$y =$ _____

3)

x	y
6	15
32	41
13	
41	
8	17

Equation:

$y =$ _____

2. Complete and determine the equation that describes each of the following tables.

1)

x	y
10	9
15	14
21	20
7	
2	

Equation:

$y =$ _____

2)

x	y
54	
13	13
62	62
9	9
19	

Equation:

$y =$ _____

3)

x	y
14	
18	13
11	
8	3
20	15

Equation:

$y =$ _____

Equations with 2 Variables

1. Complete and determine the equation that describes each of the following tables.

1)

x	y
4	8
2	
10	20
25	
3	

Equation:

$y = \underline{\textbf{2x}}$

2)

x	y
9	
1	
6	4
5	5
3	7

Equation:

$y = \underline{\textbf{10} - \textbf{x}}$

3)

x	y
10	30
2	
15	
8	
20	60

Equation:

$y = \underline{\textbf{3x}}$

2. Complete and determine the equation that describes each of the following tables.

1)

x	y
11	4
15	0
2	
9	6
13	

Equation:

$y = \underline{\textbf{15} - \textbf{x}}$

2)

x	y
4	
30	150
8	40
40	
1	5

Equation:

$y = \underline{\textbf{5x}}$

3)

x	Y
60	
8	4
18	9
24	
4	2

Equation:

$y = \underline{\dfrac{\textbf{x}}{\textbf{2}}}$

Answers

Algebra Vocabulary

1. Determine the constant(s) and the variable(s) in each algebraic expression.

	Algebraic Expressions	Constant(s)	Variable(s)
1	c + 13	13	c
2	10 - b	10	b
3	7 + m	7	m
4	3q + 1	3, 1	q
5	18p	18	p
6	5 + d + a	5	a, d
7	51	51	none
8	$\dfrac{m}{5}$	$\dfrac{1}{5}$	m
9	$\dfrac{11}{t}$ - b	11	t, b
10	$\dfrac{6}{a}$	6	a
11	8xy + 31	8, 31	x, y
12	47 + m + 9	47, 9	m
13	x + 3	3	x
14	63 + x − 11b	63, 11	x, b
15	$\dfrac{5}{4}$ (m + p)	$\dfrac{5}{4}$	m, p

Algebra Vocabulary

1. Tell whether the following is an algebraic expression or an algebaic equation.

	Algebraic (Expressions and Equations)	Algebaic Expression	Algebaic Equation
1	$3 + 2x$	X	
2	$6b = 2$		X
3	$25 - 9c$	X	
4	$7a - 22 = 11$		X
5	$102 = 4y - 3$		X
6	$5x - 17 = 18 + 54x$		X
7	$8a - 5$	X	
8	$\dfrac{t}{13} = 77$		X
9	$\dfrac{x + 1}{2} - 35$	X	
10	$\dfrac{6a}{5} + 9 = 3a$		X
11	$5p = 2p - 1$		X
12	$x^2 - 3$	X	
13	$1 = 2 - y^2$		X
14	$\dfrac{x + 1}{2}$	X	
15	$\dfrac{5x}{4} + 3 = 0$		X

Algebra Vocabulary

1. Tell whether each of the following sentences is an algebraic expression or an algebraic equation.

	Algebraic Sentences	Algebaic Expression	Algebaic Equation
1	The product of b and 5 decreased by 11	X	
2	The sum of 21 and y	X	
3	Twelve subtracted by t is 10		X
4	The product of x and 11 decreased by 51	X	
5	Twice a number less than 9 is 42		X
6	95 added to m is equal to 7		X
7	The sum of x and 35 is 61		X
8	Nineteen decreased by 3	X	
9	Thirty-seven is ten less than 8 times a number		X
10	The product of a number and 15	X	
11	84 is 6 times a number less than 12		X
12	The quotient of 42 and the sum of m and 8	X	
13	The difference between 22 and twice a number	X	
14	One third of y is 16		X
15	74 more than a number	X	

Evaluating Expressions with 1 Variable

1. Evaluate each of the following expressions for x = 7.

1. $x + 10 =$ ___17___   6. $9 + x =$ ___16___

2. $x + 23 =$ ___30___   7. $31 + x =$ ___38___

3. $x + 11 - 5 =$ ___13___   8. $x - 4 =$ ___3___

4. $x - 7 =$ ___0___   9. $3 + x - 2 =$ ___8___

5. $15 - x + 8 =$ ___16___   10. $x + 59 =$ ___66___

2. Evaluate each of the following expressions for y = 12.

1. $y + 13 =$ ___25___   6. $9 + y =$ ___21___

2. $y - 5 =$ ___7___   7. $25 + y =$ ___37___

3. $y + 9 - 2 =$ ___19___   8. $y + 33 =$ ___45___

4. $y - 9 =$ ___3___   9. $27 - y + 3 =$ ___18___

5. $6 + y - 8 =$ ___10___   10. $67 - y =$ ___55___

Evaluating Expressions with 1 Variable

1. Evaluate each of the following expressions for x = 15.

1. $x - 5 =$ __10__

2. $x + 10 =$ __25__

3. $x - 14 - 1 =$ __0__

4. $27 - x =$ __12__

5. $42 - x + 20 =$ __47__

6. $3 + x =$ __18__

7. $73 - x =$ __58__

8. $x + 2 =$ __17__

9. $1 + x - 5 =$ __11__

10. $x - 0 =$ __15__

2. Evaluate each of the following expressions for y = 21.

1. $5 + y =$ __26__

2. $96 - y - 10 =$ __65__

3. $y + 11 =$ __32__

4. $y + 61 - 19 =$ __63__

5. $42 - y =$ __21__

6. $y - 4 =$ __17__

7. $39 + y + 9 =$ __69__

8. $21 - y =$ __0__

9. $73 - y + 15 =$ __67__

10. $89 - y + 16 =$ __84__

Evaluating Expressions with 1 Variable

1. Evaluate each of the following expressions for x = 3.

1. $5x =$ ___15___

2. $6x + 9 =$ ___27___

3. $2(7x) =$ ___42___

4. $4 + 8x =$ ___28___

5. $\dfrac{x}{3} =$ ___1___

6. $3x =$ ___9___

7. $7x - 4 =$ ___17___

8. $7(4x) =$ ___84___

9. $34 - 9x =$ ___7___

10. $\dfrac{12x}{3} + 13 =$ ___25___

2. Evaluate each of the following expressions for y = 4.

1. $\dfrac{8y}{2} =$ ___16___

2. $\dfrac{36}{y} =$ ___9___

3. $5 - \dfrac{y}{4} =$ ___4___

4. $9y + 17 =$ ___53___

5. $35 - \dfrac{4y}{8} =$ ___33___

6. $\dfrac{8}{y} =$ ___2___

7. $\dfrac{24}{y} =$ ___6___

8. $\dfrac{y}{1} + 10 =$ ___14___

9. $13 - 3y =$ ___1___

10. $10 - \dfrac{3y}{2} - 4 =$ ___0___

Evaluating Expressions with 1 Variable

1. Evaluate each of the following expressions for x = 2.

1. $x^2 + 1 = $ ___5___

2. $(3x)^2 = $ ___36___

3. $x^2 - 1 = $ ___3___

4. $46 - (3x)^2 = $ ___10___

5. $4x^2 + 9 = $ ___25___

6. $3 + x^2 = $ ___7___

7. $(2x)^2 + 5 = $ ___21___

8. $6 - x^2 = $ ___2___

9. $16 - (2x)^2 = $ ___0___

10. $3x^2 - 7 = $ ___5___

2. Evaluate each of the following expressions for y = 3.

1. $\dfrac{y^2}{1} = $ ___9___

2. $4 + 5y^2 = $ ___49___

3. $5y^2 - 10 = $ ___35___

4. $y^3 = $ ___27___

5. $y^3 + 4 = $ ___31___

6. $\dfrac{2y^2}{6} = $ ___3___

7. $2y^2 + 11 = $ ___29___

8. $\dfrac{6y^2}{3} - 5 = $ ___13___

9. $2y^3 = $ ___54___

10. $y^3 - 8 = $ ___19___

Evaluating Expressions with 2 Variables

1. Evaluate each of the following expressions for x = 2 and y = 3.

1. $x + y =$ ___5___

2. $y - x =$ ___1___

3. $x + y + 2 =$ ___7___

4. $15 + y - x =$ ___16___

5. $y - 3 - x =$ ___- 2___

6. $y + x =$ ___5___

7. $x - y =$ ___- 1___

8. $x - 2 + y =$ ___3___

9. $16 + x + y =$ ___21___

10. $y - x - 1 =$ ___0___

2. Evaluate each of the following expressions for x = 4, y = 6 and z = 9.

1. $x + z =$ ___13___

2. $6 + z - x =$ ___11___

3. $x + 51 - z =$ ___50___

4. $5 + (y + z) =$ ___20___

5. $y + x - z =$ ___1___

6. $z - y =$ ___3___

7. $23 - y =$ ___17___

8. $x + y + z =$ ___19___

9. $12 - (z - y) =$ ___9___

10. $x + z - y =$ ___7___

Evaluating Expressions with 2 Variables

1. Evaluate each of the following expressions for x = 8 and y = 2.

1. $3x + y =$ **26**

6. $5y + x =$ **18**

2. $10y - x =$ **12**

7. $2x - 8y =$ **0**

3. $4x + 3y - 20 =$ **18**

8. $6x - 15 + 2y =$ **13**

4. $21 - y - 2x =$ **3**

9. $16 + \dfrac{x}{2} + 5y =$ **30**

5. $\dfrac{y}{2} - 1 + x =$ **8**

10. $\dfrac{x + y}{2} - 6 =$ **-1**

2. Evaluate each of the following expressions for x = 10, y = 5 and z = 7.

1. $xy =$ **50**

6. $2yz - 1 =$ **69**

2. $\dfrac{x}{y} =$ **2**

7. $2xy + 3 =$ **103**

3. $\dfrac{4y}{z - 5} =$ **10**

8. $x - 2y - 4 =$ **-4**

4. $\dfrac{7x}{z} + 5 =$ **15**

9. $\dfrac{x}{z - y} - 5 =$ **0**

5. $100xz + 5 =$ **7005**

10. $\dfrac{xz}{y} + \dfrac{2yz}{x} =$ **21**

Evaluating Expressions with 2 Variables

1. Evaluate each of the following expressions for $x = 3$ and $y = 5$.

1. $x^2 + y = $ ___14___

2. $5xy - 1 = $ ___74___

3. $2x^2 + 3y^2 = $ ___93___

4. $(x - y)^2 = $ ___4___

5. $\dfrac{x^2}{3} - 1 = $ ___2___

6. $5y^2 - 2x = $ ___119___

7. $7(2x - y) = $ ___7___

8. $x^2 - 1 - y^2 = $ ___-17___

9. $100xy - 500 = $ ___1000___

10. $\dfrac{x + y^2}{4} - 7 = $ ___0___

2. Evaluate each of the following expressions for $x = 3$, $y = 12$ and $z = 8$.

1. $2x^2y = $ ___216___

2. $x^3 - 40 = $ ___-13___

3. $\dfrac{yz}{x + 1} = $ ___24___

4. $3x^2 + 2y - z = $ ___43___

5. $xyz = $ ___288___

6. $200xz = $ ___4800___

7. $(2x + 3y)^2 = $ ___1764___

8. $\dfrac{xz}{y} + \dfrac{yz}{x} = $ ___34___

9. $\dfrac{z^2}{x^2 - 1} - 10 = $ ___-2___

10. $(x - y)^2 - z^2 = $ ___17___

Writing Algebraic Expressions

1. Determine what operation is indicated by each of the following words.

	Words	Add (+)	Subtract (−)	Multiply (X)	Divide (÷)
1)	Difference		X		
2)	Quotient				X
3)	Increased by	X			
4)	Decreased by		X		
5)	Of			X	
6)	Sum	X			
7)	Subtracted from		X		
8)	Distributed among				X
9)	Product			X	
10)	In addition to	X			
11)	Double			X	
12)	Less		X		
13)	More than	X			

Writing Algebraic Expressions

1. Determine what operation is indicated by each of the following words.

	Words	Add (+)	Subtract (−)	Multiply (X)	Divide (÷)
14)	Divided by				X
15)	Fewer than		X		
16)	Total	X			
17)	Per				X
18)	Minus		X		
19)	Multiplied by			X	
20)	Plus	X			
21)	Twice			X	
22)	Less than		X		
23)	Times			X	
24)	Take away		X		
25)	Into				X

Writing Algebraic Expressions

1. Rewrite each of the following phrases as an algebraic expression.

	Phrase	Algebraic Expression
1.	Nine decreased by b	$9 - b$
2.	Eleven less than x	$x - 11$
3.	y increased by 5	$y + 5$
4.	a less than 21	$21 - a$
5.	x divided by 2	$\dfrac{x}{2}$
6.	Ninteen multiplied by a number y	$19y$
7.	The product of 13 and f	$13f$
8.	Thirty-one less than t	$t - 31$

2. Rewrite each of the following phrases as an algebraic expression.

	Phrase	Algebraic Expression
1.	Five more than m	$m + 5$
2.	x diminished by 42	$x - 42$
3.	Three-fourths of y	$\dfrac{3}{4}y$
4.	Thrice a number x	$3x$
5.	The quotient of m and 11	$\dfrac{m}{11}$
6.	The sum of 81 and d	$81 + d$
7.	Seventy-nine less than x	$x - 79$
8.	Ninety-eight more than f	$f + 98$

Writing Algebraic Expressions

1. Rewrite each of the following phrases as an algebraic expression.

	Phrase	Algebraic Expression
1.	The difference between m and 17	$m - 17$
2.	The product of 35 and x	$35x$
3.	t less than 52	$52 - t$
4.	x increased by y	$x + y$
5.	8 times p	$8p$
6.	11 more than b	$b + 11$
7.	The sum of x and 63	$x + 63$
8.	The ratio of 22 and y	$\dfrac{22}{y}$

2. Rewrite each of the following phrases as an algebraic expression.

	Phrase	Algebraic Expression
1.	Twice a number d	$2d$
2.	The sum of b and 46	$b + 46$
3.	Exceeds x by 71	$x + 71$
4.	The quotient of t and 92	$\dfrac{t}{92}$
5.	y reduced by 21	$y - 21$
6.	The ratio of 18 and b	$\dfrac{18}{b}$
7.	The difference between 102 and m	$102 - m$
8.	x less than y	$y - x$

Writing Algebraic Expressions

1. Rewrite each of the following phrases as an algebraic expression.

	Phrase	Algebraic Expression
1.	The product of x and 7 increased by 12	$7x + 12$
2.	The quotient of y and sum of t and 4	$\dfrac{y}{t + 4}$
3.	21 greater than x	$x + 21$
4.	a subtracted by 10	$a - 10$
5.	Seventy-four increased by nine times x	$9x + 74$
6.	Twenty-six less than three times m	$3m - 26$
7.	Forty-seven more than Six times q	$6q + 47$
8.	Two-thirds of p	$\dfrac{2}{3}p$

2. Rewrite each of the following phrases as an algebraic expression.

	Phrase	Algebraic Expression
1.	Two times y, decreased by 54	$2y - 54$
2.	Square of m	m^2
3.	Nineteen decreased by the product of 4 and t	$19 - 4t$
4.	Eighty-five less than the square of x	$x^2 - 85$
5.	The quotient of 22 and the sum of 15 and b	$\dfrac{22}{15 + b}$
6.	Three times the product of x and y	$3xy$
7.	The sum of 21 and the quotient of t and 8	$21 + \dfrac{t}{8}$
8.	The product of 16 and square of x	$16x^2$

Simplifying Expressions

1. Simplify each of the following expressions.

1. $3x + x =$ _____ **4x** _____

2. $5x - x =$ _____ **4x** _____

3. $4y + 7y =$ _____ **11y** _____

4. $13x - 8x - 3x + 13 - 11 =$ _____ **2x + 2** _____

5. $6y - 2 + 10y + 7 - 20y - 1 =$ _____ **– 4y + 4** _____

6. $2x + 5 + x =$ _____ **3x + 5** _____

7. $7x + 10 - x =$ _____ **6x + 10** _____

8. $9x - 5x =$ _____ **4x** _____

9. $25 - 2x + 3x =$ _____ **25 + x** _____

10. $12x - 5 + 5x =$ _____ **17x – 5** _____

2. Simplify each of the following expressions.

1. $9 + 3y + 8 + 5y - 2 + 4y =$ _____ **12y + 15** _____

2. $5x + 1 + 2x + 7 - 7x - 8 =$ _____ **0** _____

3. $10x + 8 - 6x + 5 + 2x + 1 =$ _____ **6x + 14** _____

4. $4 - 5 + 2x - 4x - 6 - 9x =$ _____ **– 11x – 7** _____

5. $5x + 8x - 3x + 9 - 17 =$ _____ **10x – 8** _____

6. $9y + 5 - 9y =$ _____ **5** _____

7. $4 + 5x - 4 =$ _____ **5x** _____

8. $19x - 21x =$ _____ **– 2x** _____

9. $31x + x =$ _____ **32x** _____

10. $-x + 22x =$ _____ **21x** _____

Simplifying Expressions

1. Simplify each of the following expressions then evaluate it for x = 4.

1. $6x + 5x =$ __11x__ $=$ __44__

2. $12x - 8x =$ __4x__ $=$ __16__

3. $9x - 10x + 1 =$ __−x + 1__ $=$ __−3__

4. $15x - 10x - 20 =$ __5x − 20__ $=$ __0__

5. $7x - 2 + x =$ __8x − 2__ $=$ __30__

6. $8 + 20x - 17x =$ __8 + 3x__ $=$ __20__

7. $-x - 6 + 3x =$ __2x − 6__ $=$ __2__

8. $32x - 21x =$ __11x__ $=$ __44__

9. $100 - 20x + 4 + =$ __104 − 20x__ $=$ __24__

10. $18x - 12 + 2x =$ __20x − 12__ $=$ __68__

2. Simplify each of the following expressions then evaluate it for y = 3.

1. $21y - 7y + 15 - 3y - 7 + 12 =$ __11y + 20__ $=$ __53__

2. $4y + 20 + 10y - 6 - 5y - 11 =$ __9y + 3__ $=$ __30__

3. $32y - 15 + 5y + 12 - 30y + 3 - y =$ __6y__ $=$ __18__

4. $30 - 8y - 20 + 2y - 4y + 13 - 3 + y =$ __20 − 9y__ $=$ __−7__

5. $54y + 21 - 4y - 40 - 30y - 41 =$ __20y − 60__ $=$ __0__

6. $2y - 10 + 40y - 2y + 100 - 1 =$ __40y − 89__ $=$ __31__

7. $100y - 20 - 40 - 40y - 30y + 45 =$ __30y − 15__ $=$ __75__

Solving One-Step Equations

1. Solve each of the following equations. Answers should be expressed as: x = ____

1. $x + 1 = 2$; x = __1__

2. $x + 5 = 10$; x = __5__

3. $2 + x = 16$; x = __14__

4. $x + 1000 = 1251$; x = __251__

5. $325 + x = 402$; x = __77__

6. $x + 100 = 250$; x = __150__

7. $x + 12 = 25$; x = __13__

8. $25 + x = 63$; x = __38__

9. $x + 14 = 14$; x = __0__

10. $47 + x = 50$; x = __3__

2. Solve each of the following equations. Answers should be expressed as: x = ____

1. $x - 1 = 3$; x = __4__

2. $x - 9 = 1$; x = __10__

3. $x - 7 = 14$; x = __21__

4. $x - 105 = 125$; x = __230__

5. $x - 2500 = 55$; x = __2555__

6. $x - 30 = 45$; x = __75__

7. $x - 2 = 45$; x = __47__

8. $x - 11 = 5$; x = __16__

9. $x - 1004 = 16$; x = __1020__

10. $x - 3 = 1007$; x = __1010__

Solving One-Step Equations

1. Solve each of the following equations. Answers should be expressed as: x = ____

1. $2x = 4$; x = _2_

2. $4x = 12$; x = _3_

3. $5x = 30$; x = _6_

4. $7x = 7$; x = _1_

5. $10x = 400$; x = _40_

6. $9x = 81$; x = _9_

7. $11x = 55$; x = _5_

8. $6x = 24$; x = _4_

9. $3x = 90$; x = _30_

10. $15x = 150$; x = _10_

2. Solve each of the following equations. Answers should be expressed as: x = ____

1. $\dfrac{x}{2} = 1$; x = _2_

2. $\dfrac{x}{3} = 4$; x = _12_

3. $12x = 48$; x = _4_

4. $\dfrac{2x}{3} = 4$; x = _6_

5. $50x = 1000$; x = _20_

6. $\dfrac{x}{5} = 10$; x = _50_

7. $\dfrac{3x}{7} = 6$; x = _14_

8. $22x = 110$; x = _5_

9. $\dfrac{14x}{3} = 28$; x = _6_

10. $\dfrac{8x}{11} = 32$; x = _44_

Solving 2 Step Equations

1. Solve each of the following equations and show your work.

1) $2x + 4 = 12$

   $x = 4$

2) $1 + 3x = 22$

   $x = 7$

3) $5x - 3 = 42$

   $x = 9$

4) $42 - 4x = 2$

   $x = 8$

5) $12x + 62 = 86$

   $x = 2$

6) $31 + 18x = 121$

   $x = 5$

7) $22x - 7 = 15$

   $x = 1$

8) $13x - 11 = 28$

   $x = 3$

9) $19 + 8x = 99$

   $x = 10$

10) $15x + 63 = 153$

   $x = 6$

Solving 2 Sided Equations

1. Solve each of the following equations and show your work.

1) $2x + 1 = x + 3$

$x = 2$

2) $3x + 20 = 45 + 2x$

$x = 25$

3) $4x - 3 = 2x + 7$

$x = 5$

4) $x + 1 = 3 - x$

$x = 1$

5) $10 - x = 17 - 2x$

$x = 7$

6) $63 - 5x = 90 - 8x$

$x = 9$

7) $2x + 21 = 29 - 2x$

$x = 2$

8) $3 - x = 20 - 2x$

$x = 17$

9) $92 + 6x = 112 + 4x$

$x = 10$

10) $6 + 8x - 32 = 5x + 19$

$x = 15$

Solving 2 Sided Equations

1. Solve each of the following equations and show your work.

1) $5 + 4x - 1 = 2x + 34$

   $x = 15$

2) $11 - 7x - 10 = 152 - 8x - 51$

   $x = 100$

3) $7 + 21x - 101 = 16x - 84$

   $x = 2$

4) $9x - 33 = 69 + 4x - 47$

   $x = 11$

5) $7x - 10 = 30 - 3x$

   $x = 4$

6) $2x - 49 + 25 = 112 + x - 87$

   $x = 49$

7) $91 + 13x - 10 = 30 - 7x + 409$

   $x = 27$

8) $100 + 125x = 3,600 + 25x$

   $x = 35$

9) $1 - x = 95 - 2x$

   $x = 94$

10) $10 + x = 2,420 - x$

   $x = 1,205$

Equations with 2 Variables

1. Complete each of the following tables.

1) $y = x$

x	y
1	1
2	2
3	3
4	4
5	5
6	6
7	7

2) $y = x + 1$

x	y
5	6
1	2
7	8
9	10
4	5
2	3
8	9

3) $y = x + 10$

x	y
5	15
1	11
7	17
9	19
4	14
2	12
8	18

2. Complete each of the following tables.

1) $y = x - 1$

x	y
2	1
11	10
8	7
13	12
1	0
5	4
19	18

2) $y = x - 4$

x	y
8	4
9	5
5	1
4	0
12	8
10	6
20	16

3) $y = x - 12$

x	y
25	13
12	0
32	20
17	5
13	1
42	30
102	90

Equations with 2 Variables

1. Complete each of the following tables.

1) $y = 2x$

x	y
15	30
8	16
21	42
35	70
4	8
18	36
50	100

2) $y = 3x + 2$

x	y
4	14
15	47
42	128
9	20
1	5
0	2
16	50

3) $y = 2x + 15$

x	y
31	77
10	35
25	65
19	53
52	119
8	31
12	39

2. Complete each of the following tables.

1) $y = 4x - 2$

x	y
2	6
9	34
1	2
10	38
62	246
85	338
5	18

2) $y = 5x - 20$

x	y
16	60
4	0
30	130
6	10
44	200
14	50
5	5

3) $y = 100x - 20$

x	y
2	180
5	480
6	580
1	80
3	280
12	1180
8	780

Equations with 2 Variables

1. Complete each of the following tables.

1) $x + y = 16$

x	y
12	4
4	12
1	15
10	6
6	10
14	2
2	14

2) $y + x = 25$

x	y
20	5
12	13
25	0
9	16
18	7
5	20
24	1

3) $y - x = 7$

x	y
72	79
18	25
4	11
57	64
19	26
1	8
95	102

2. Complete each of the following tables.

1) $y - 9 = x$

x	y
29	38
10	19
38	47
7	16
1	10
13	22
55	64

2) $y + 6 = 2x$

x	y
4	2
63	120
19	32
10	14
50	94
8	10
3	0

3) $y - 2 = x + 1$

x	y
3	6
11	14
50	53
125	128
2	5
73	76
83	86

Equations with 2 Variables

1. Complete and determine the equation that describes each of the following tables.

1)

x	y
3	5
10	12
5	7
1	3
25	27

Equation:

$y = \underline{x + 2}$

2)

x	y
11	15
7	11
21	25
4	8
2	6

Equation:

$y = \underline{x + 4}$

3)

x	y
6	15
32	41
13	22
41	50
8	17

Equation:

$y = \underline{x + 9}$

2. Complete and determine the equation that describes each of the following tables.

1)

x	y
10	9
15	14
21	20
7	6
2	1

Equation:

$y = \underline{x - 1}$

2)

x	y
54	54
13	13
62	62
9	9
19	19

Equation:

$y = \underline{x}$

3)

x	y
14	9
18	13
11	6
8	3
20	15

Equation:

$y = \underline{x - 5}$

Equations with 2 Variables

1. Complete and determine the equation that describes each of the following tables.

1)

x	y
4	8
2	4
10	20
25	50
3	6

Equation:

$y = $ __2x__

2)

x	y
9	1
1	9
6	4
5	5
3	7

Equation:

$y = $ __10 − x__

3)

x	y
10	30
2	6
15	45
8	24
20	60

Equation:

$y = $ __3x__

2. Complete and determine the equation that describes each of the following tables.

1)

x	y
11	4
15	0
2	13
9	6
13	2

Equation:

$y = $ __15 − x__

2)

x	y
4	20
30	150
8	40
40	200
1	5

Equation:

$y = $ __5x__

3)

x	y
60	30
8	4
18	9
24	12
4	2

Equation:

$y = \dfrac{x}{2}$

Made in United States
North Haven, CT
17 October 2022

25587512R00033